Background

Alimony is a payment to or for a spouse or former spouse under a divorce or separation instrument.[1] Individuals who pay alimony can deduct the amount paid from income on their tax return to reduce the amount of tax they must pay. Conversely, individuals who receive alimony must claim the amount received as income on their tax return.[2] More than 1.7 million tax returns included an alimony deduction claim in Tax Years[3] 2008 through 2010. Of those, approximately 1.2 million tax returns (71 percent) were filed electronically (e-filed) and 520,000 tax returns (31 percent) were filed on paper.[4] Figure 1 provides details of the total number of individuals claiming an alimony deduction and the amount claimed for Tax Years 2008 through 2010.

Figure 1: Alimony Deductions – Tax Years 2008 Through 2010

	Tax Year 2008	**Tax Year 2009**	**Tax Year 2010**	**Total**
Tax Returns	577,003	573,904	567,887	1,718,794
Alimony Deduction Claimed	$9.9 billion	$10.4 billion	$10 billion	$30.3 billion

Source: Treasury Inspector General for Tax Administration (TIGTA) analysis of the Internal Revenue Service (IRS) Individual Return Transaction File[5] for Tax Years 2008 through 2010.

Processing tax returns with alimony deductions

Individuals who pay alimony report the amount paid as a deduction on Line 31a (Alimony Paid) on Form 1040, *U.S. Individual Income Tax Return*. These individuals are required to include the Taxpayer Identification Number (TIN)[6] of the recipient on Line 31b of their tax return. Figure 2 provides an illustration of Form 1040 Line 31.

---

[1] Divorce or separation instrument includes a decree of divorce, a written separation agreement, or a decree or any type of court order requiring a spouse to make payments for the support or maintenance of the other spouse.

[2] Individuals who receive alimony income are not required to file a tax return if their total income is below the minimum income required to have a tax return filing requirement. In Tax Year 2010, individuals who had less than $9,350 in income ($18,700 if married filing jointly) were not required to file a tax return.

[3] A 12-month accounting period for keeping records on income and expenses used as the basis for calculating the annual taxes due. For most individual taxpayers, the tax year is synonymous with the calendar year.

[4] Percentages do not equal 100 percent due to rounding.

[5] A database the IRS maintains that contains information on the individual tax returns it receives.

[6] A nine-digit number assigned to taxpayers for identification purposes. Depending upon the nature of the taxpayer, the TIN is an Employer Identification Number, a Social Security Number, or an Individual TIN.

Figure 2: Tax Year 2012 Form 1040 Line 31 – Alimony Paid

Adjusted Gross Income	23	Educator expenses	23		
	24	Certain business expenses of reservists, performing artists, and fee-basis government officials. Attach Form 2106 or 2106-EZ	24		
	25	Health savings account deduction. Attach Form 8889	25		
	26	Moving expenses. Attach Form 3903	26		
	27	Deductible part of self-employment tax. Attach Schedule SE	27		
	28	Self-employed SEP, SIMPLE, and qualified plans	28		
	29	Self-employed health insurance deduction	29		
	30	Penalty on early withdrawal of savings	30		
➡	31a	Alimony paid b Recipient's SSN ▶	31a		
	32	IRA deduction	32		
	33	Student loan interest deduction	33		
	34	Tuition and fees. Attach Form 8917	34		
	35	Domestic production activities deduction. Attach Form 8903	35		
	36	Add lines 23 through 35		36	
	37	Subtract line 36 from line 22. This is your adjusted gross income ▶		37	

For Disclosure, Privacy Act, and Paperwork Reduction Act Notice, see separate instructions.   Cat. No. 11320B   Form **1040** (2012)

Source: Tax Year 2012 Form 1040.

The IRS rejects an e-filed tax return claiming an alimony deduction if the recipient TIN is missing or incomplete.[7] As of June 19, 2013, the IRS rejected 872 e-filed Tax Year 2012 tax returns for missing or incomplete recipient TINs. For paper-filed tax returns with missing or incomplete recipient TINs,[8] the IRS will suspend the processing of the tax return and correspond with the taxpayer to obtain a valid TIN.[9]

This review was performed in the Wage and Investment Division Submission Processing function located in Cincinnati, Ohio; the Small Business/Self-Employed Division Examination function located in Washington, D.C.; and the IRS campuses[10] located in Andover, Massachusetts; Austin, Texas; and Ogden, Utah, during the period August 2012 through August 2013. We conducted this performance audit in accordance with generally accepted government auditing standards. Those standards require that we plan and perform the audit to obtain sufficient, appropriate evidence to provide a reasonable basis for our findings and conclusions based on our audit objective. We believe that the evidence obtained provides a reasonable basis for our findings and conclusions based on our audit objective. Detailed

---

[7] An incomplete recipient TIN is fewer than nine digits or does not fall within the valid range of numbers issued by the Social Security Administration.

[8] The IRS was unable to provide us with the number of paper-filed tax returns with a missing or incomplete TIN that it suspended during processing to correspond with the taxpayer to obtain a corrected TIN. The IRS indicated that this figure could not be provided because this letter is also used for other issues requiring correspondence with the taxpayer.

[9] A "valid TIN" is a TIN that matches the information contained on the National Account Profile, which is a compilation of selected entity data from various master files and the Social Security Administration.

[10] The data processing arm of the IRS. The campuses process paper and electronic submissions, correct errors, and forward data to the Computing Centers for analysis and posting to taxpayer accounts.

information on our audit objective, scope, and methodology is presented in Appendix I. Major contributors to the report are listed in Appendix II.

Results of Review

Processes Have Not Been Developed to Address the Majority of Discrepancies Between Alimony Deductions Claimed and Income Reported

Our analysis of the 567,887 Tax Year 2010 tax returns with an alimony deduction claim identified 266,190 (47 percent) tax returns[11] in which it appears individuals claimed alimony deductions for which the corresponding income was either not reported on a recipient's tax return or the amount of alimony income reported did not agree with the deduction taken. As such, there is a discrepancy of more than $2.3 billion in deductions claimed without corresponding income reported.

Analysis of the tax return filings for the recipient listed by the payer as receiving the alimony income claimed as a deduction on the 266,190 tax returns identified:

- 222,895 (84 percent) tax returns filed by the recipient.

- 36,795 (14 percent) with no tax return filed by the recipient; however, the amount of alimony deducted as being paid would have required the recipient to file a tax return.[12]

- 6,500 (2 percent) tax returns for which we were unable to determine if the income was reported as the recipient TIN provided on the payer tax return was either missing or not valid.

The Internal Revenue Code[13] states that alimony is deductible by the payer and must be included in the spouse's or former spouse's income. Figure 3 provides an analysis of alimony income reported by recipients whom the payer claiming the deduction listed as having received alimony income.

---

[11] This figure is an estimate based on our review of Tax Year 2010 tax returns as follows: 100 percent of the 447,975 e-filed tax returns claiming an alimony deduction, 100 percent of the 84,562 paper tax returns claiming an alimony deduction above the amount for which the IRS will capture the recipient TIN listed on the tax return, and a statistically valid sample of 138 of the 35,350 paper tax returns that claimed an alimony deduction below the amount for which the IRS will capture the recipient TIN listed on the tax return. See Appendix I for the details of our analysis.

[12] In Tax Year 2010, individuals who had less than $9,350 in income ($18,700 if married filing jointly) were not required to file a tax return.

[13] Internal Revenue Code § 215.

Figure 3: Analysis of Income Reported by Alleged Recipients for Tax Year 2010

	Tax Returns	Deductions Claimed by Payer	Associated Income Not Reported by Recipient
Tax Return Filed by Recipient	**222,895**	**$3.3 billion**	**$1.4 billion**
Alimony Income Was Not Reported	*122,870*	*$1.1 billion*	*$1.1 billion*
Alimony Income Reported Was Less Than Deduction Claimed[14]	*75,383*	*$1.7 billion*	*$375.2 million*
Alimony Income Reported Was More Than Deduction Claimed	*24,642*	*$469.2 million*	*- $74.6 million*
No Tax Return Filed by Recipient	**36,795**	**$937.2 million**	**$937.2 million**
Unable to Determine If Income Was Reported – Recipient TIN Missing or Not Valid	**6,500**	**$95.7 million**	**Unable to Determine**
TOTAL	**266,190**	**$4.3 billion**	**$2.3 billion**

Source: *TIGTA analysis of Tax Year 2010 tax returns processed through December 31, 2011.*

Apart from examining a small number of tax returns, the IRS has no processes or procedures to address the alimony reporting compliance gap

Each year subsequent to the processing of tax returns, the IRS Examination function performs a match of tax returns with alimony deduction claims to associated recipient TIN tax returns. This match is performed to identify tax returns for examination that have a high risk for alimony deduction noncompliance. For those tax returns selected, the IRS performs an examination to determine if the deduction is valid. If the deduction is validated, then the associated recipient TIN tax return is reviewed to determine if the alimony income was reported correctly.

However, the IRS will select for examination only those tax returns in which the alimony deduction claim is above a certain dollar amount. For Tax Year 2010, this prevented ****2****** of the 266,190 tax returns we identified as having a discrepancy between the amount deducted and the amount reported as income from being considered for audit selection. These ***2*** tax returns had more than $156 million in alimony deductions claimed for which no income was reported on a recipient tax return (the estimated associated reduction in tax liability was more than $45 million).

---

[14] These returns may include instances in which individuals pay alimony to more than one recipient.

Further limiting the effectiveness of IRS efforts to address alimony deduction and income discrepancies is that the number of examinations the IRS conducts is based on the allocation of limited examination resources. For example, the IRS selected only 10,870 of the remaining 188,468 Tax Year 2010 returns for examination.

Examination selection filters may inappropriately exclude tax returns with high-risk characteristics

Once the IRS performs the match of tax returns with alimony deduction claims to associated recipient TIN tax returns, it applies exclusionary filters to better identify those high-risk tax returns it will consider for examination. These filters are designed to exclude tax returns with certain characteristics that the IRS believes represent a low risk of alimony deduction/income noncompliance. The IRS has developed seven filters to assist it in identifying tax returns with the highest risk of alimony noncompliance. However, our review of the filter criteria identified three filters that we believe may inappropriately exclude some alimony deduction claims that in fact have high-risk characteristics from being selected for examination.[15] Figure 4 provides an overview of the questionable examination filters we identified.

Figure 4: Filters That May Inappropriately Exclude Tax Returns With Questionable Alimony Deduction Claims From Being Selected for Examination

Description	Reason the Filter Inappropriately Excludes Tax Returns With High-Risk Characteristics
****************2****************** ****************2********* .	********************************2******************************** *********2************ .
***********2***************************** ********2**********	********************************2******************************** ********************************2******************************** ********************************2******************************** ***********************************2******************************** ************************* 16 *2******************* ****************************2*************************
****************2********************* ****************2********************* ***********2**************	********************************2******************************** ********************************2******************************** ********************************2******************************** ********************************2******************************** *******************2****************** .

Source: TIGTA analysis of IRS alimony program examination filters.

---

[15] The filters would only prevent the returns from being examined for the alimony deduction; the returns could still be considered for other examinations.
[16] **********************************2** **********************************2*****************************.

We notified the IRS of our concerns regarding the examination filters in February 2013. IRS management indicated that studies show that examining tax returns selected by these filters is less cost effective than tax returns with other types of potential reporting errors. However, the IRS was unable to provide us these studies.

Soft notices could help address the discrepancies between alimony deductions claimed and income reported

Apart from examining a small number of tax returns, the IRS generally has no processes or procedures to address this substantial compliance gap. The use of soft notices could significantly expand the IRS's ability to address the discrepancies between alimony deducted and the amounts claimed by recipients as income. For example, soft notices could alert individuals to potential errors on their tax return related to the claiming of an alimony deduction or the nonreporting of alimony income as required.

The IRS uses soft notices to address noncompliance in other areas of the tax system. The notices commonly provide individuals with information specific to the eligibility or reporting requirements related to the potential error and suggest the filing of a Form 1040X, *Amended U.S. Individual Income Tax Return*, if an error has occurred. For example, in September 2010, we reported that the IRS issues notices to individuals involved in multiple dependent TIN uses.[17] These notices are issued to individuals who have used dependent TINs to obtain tax deductions or credits on their return when those same dependent TINs have already been used on other taxpayers' returns.

The IRS estimates the current cost to print and mail a soft notice as $0.57. If issuance of the notice results in a contact from the individual receiving the notice or an amended tax return being filed to correct an error, the cost to address the individual's response could be up to $33.21. A May 2009 IRS study on the effectiveness of the notices sent to individuals with multiple uses of the same dependent TIN found that 10 percent of the individuals who received a notice amended their original tax return and 92 percent changed their filing behavior in the subsequent tax year. An example of a soft notice can be found in Appendix V.

IRS management raised concerns with the use of soft notices to address the discrepancies between alimony deducted and income claimed because it would create additional work for which the IRS does not have the resources to address. For example, additional resources would be needed to process the amended tax returns generated by the notice. Nonetheless, the alternative is to permit the omission of income or overclaims of deductions even in those instances when the IRS has evidence of the problem. This would be at odds with the IRS's general practices when the IRS has information from a payer (such as a Form 1099) indicating

---

[17] TIGTA, Ref. No. 2010-40-117, *Multiple Use of Taxpayer Identification Numbers Continues to Result in Significant Erroneous Exemptions and Credits* (Sept. 2010).

that a recipient omitted income. Moreover, it would forego an even greater benefit, as shown in the 2009 IRS study, that the majority of individuals receiving a soft notice change their behavior in a subsequent tax year.

The results of examinations of returns with this issue are further indication that additional action is needed. Examinations show that the rate of noncompliance is high. Most of the tax returns examined result in an adjustment of a deduction taken or an assessment related to income not reported. As of December 31, 2013, the IRS closed examinations on 8,837 of the 10,870 tax returns that it selected for examination and adjusted deductions of more than $26 million on 4,950 (56 percent) of the 8,837 tax returns. The examinations of the payers who claimed the deductions led to an additional 2,075 examinations of the alimony recipients' tax returns to date, 1,639 of these have been completed and closed, which resulted in assessments of more than $5 million on 1,372 (83 percent) of the recipients' tax returns.

Based on the results of completed IRS examinations, we estimate that noncompliance with regard to those returns not selected for examination totals more than $351 million in unreported tax resulting from an erroneous deduction or unreported income. Over five years, this could result in more than $1.7 billion in unreported tax. Figure 5 provides a breakdown of the estimated revenue loss resulting from this substantial compliance gap.[18]

Figure 5: Estimated Revenue Loss From Unexamined Erroneous Alimony Deductions and Unreported Alimony Income[19]

	Tax Returns	Total Alimony	Tax Effect
Unexamined Alimony Deductions	139,339	$1.19 billion	$274.1 million
Unexamined Alimony Income	90,869	$777.7 million	$77.7 million
Total	**230,208**	**$1.97 billion**	**$351.8 million**

Source: TIGTA analysis of Tax Year 2010 tax returns processed through December 31, 2011, and IRS closed examination statistics.

---

[18] See Appendix IV for details of our computation.
[19] Numbers may not total due to rounding.

Recommendations

The Commissioner, Small Business/Self-Employed Division, should work with the Commissioner, Wage and Investment Division, to:

Recommendation 1: Evaluate current examination selection filters to ensure that the filters do not inappropriately exclude potentially high-risk tax returns with questionable alimony deduction claims.

> ***Management's Response:*** The IRS agreed with this recommendation. The IRS enhanced filters for Tax Year 2013 (Filing Season 2014). The Small Business/ Self-Employed Division will continue to work with the Wage and Investment Division to review the current alimony filters and make improvements as necessary.

Recommendation 2: Develop a strategy that adequately addresses the significant alimony compliance gap. This strategy should include determining the net benefit of using soft notices as an alternative approach to address this issue, as well as actions the IRS plans to take with regard to individuals who continue to misreport alimony deductions and/or income.

> ***Management's Response:*** The IRS agreed with this recommendation. The IRS currently has procedures in place to address the alimony compliance gap and will continue to review and improve its strategy as warranted. The IRS also agreed that sending soft notices may be a valid approach in certain circumstances. However, the IRS stated that resource constraints limit the IRS's ability to test their impact at this time. Instead, the IRS will continue to improve its current strategy including making changes to the examination filters.

> ***Office of Audit Comment:*** Although the IRS agreed with our recommendation, the IRS disagreed with our outcome measure of $1.7 billion in potential revenue protected because it does not have the ability to audit all the tax returns cited in our report. However, we did not recommend that the IRS examine more tax returns. We recommended that the IRS develop a strategy, including the use of less costly non-examination processes, to more adequately address the alimony reporting gap. Such a strategy should ensure the most efficient use of resources to achieve the most significant improvement in taxpayer compliance possible. Our outcome measure reflects the potential unreported revenue we believe the IRS could address by developing such a strategy.

Processes Do Not Identify All Alimony Deduction Claims Without a Valid Recipient Taxpayer Identification Number

IRS processes do not identify all alimony deduction claims in which the payer did not provide a valid recipient TIN as required. Analysis of the 567,887 Tax Year 2010 returns that claimed an alimony deduction identified an estimated 6,500 tax returns claiming more than $95 million in alimony deductions that the IRS did not identify in which the recipient TIN was either missing or invalid. These individuals may have inappropriately reduced their Tax Year 2010 tax liability by more than $27 million. Figure 6 provides the details of our analysis of alimony recipient TINs for Tax Year 2010 returns.

Figure 6: Estimated Alimony Deductions Claimed With a Missing or Invalid Recipient TIN for Tax Year 2010

	Number of Tax Returns	Potentially Erroneous Alimony Deductions	Estimated Tax Effect
Tax Returns With Alimony Deductions	**6,500**	**$95.7 million**	**$27.5 million**
Tax Returns With a Missing Recipient TIN	*3,771*	*$59.9 million*	*$18.1 million*
Tax Returns With an Invalid Recipient TIN	*2,729*	*$35.8 million*	*$9.4 million*

Source: TIGTA analysis of IRS Individual Return Transaction File information for Tax Year 2010.

Internal Revenue Code Section 215 states:

> *(1) Any individual receiving alimony or separate maintenance payments is required to furnish such individual's taxpayer identification number to the individual making such payments, and*

> *(2) The individual making such payments is required to include such taxpayer identification number on such individual's return for the taxable year in which such payments are made.*

The IRS does not verify whether a recipient TIN is provided as required for alimony deduction claims filed on a paper tax return when the amount claimed is below a certain dollar tolerance. In addition, the IRS is not using the National Account Profile[20] to ensure that the recipient TIN provided on both paper and e-filed tax returns is valid. The IRS uses the National Account Profile to validate the primary taxpayer, spouse, and dependent TINs as well as TINs used to claim tax benefits such as the Earned Income Tax Credit, the Child Tax Credit, and the American Opportunity Tax Credit.

---

[20] The National Account Profile is a compilation of selected entity data from various master files and the Social Security Administration.

Due to errors in IRS processing instructions, penalties for missing or invalid alimony recipient TINs are rarely assessed

The purpose of penalties is to encourage voluntary compliance by imposing consequences for noncompliance. The Internal Revenue Code authorizes the IRS to assess a $50 penalty when an individual does not provide a valid alimony recipient TIN as required. Internal Revenue Code Section 6723 states:

> *In the case of a failure by any person to comply with a specified information reporting requirement on or before the time prescribed therefore, such person shall pay a penalty of $50 for each such failure, but the total amount imposed on such person for all such failures during any calendar year shall not exceed $100,000.*

Our analysis of the estimated 6,500 tax returns we identified with a missing or invalid recipient TIN found that the IRS assessed the recipient TIN penalty on only 20 of the 6,500 tax returns. In addition, for those assessed, the amount was $5 instead of $50 (the IRS could not provide an explanation as to why the $5 was assessed on these 20 accounts). As a result, the IRS did not assess $324,900 in penalties for a missing or invalid recipient TIN. We estimate that the IRS may not assess more than $1.6 million in applicable penalties over the next five years as a result of weaknesses in its processes to identify missing or invalid recipient TINs.

In December 2012, we notified the IRS that the penalty for not providing a valid recipient TIN was not being assessed. The IRS agreed and indicated that this was due to incorrect processing instructions. Processing guidelines correctly instructed IRS employees to notate the tax return when the recipient TIN was missing. However, the instructions did not direct employees to code the tax return so that it would be forwarded to the IRS Error Resolution function for correspondence with the taxpayer and assessment of the penalty if warranted.

IRS management indicated that the processing instructions were revised on May 22, 2013, to correct the error. However, our review of a judgmental sample[21] of 60 tax returns processed between June 28 and July 18, 2013, that met the IRS's existing penalty criteria found that none of the taxpayers had been assessed a penalty even though the recipient TIN was missing or invalid and the amount of the deduction was above the examination dollar tolerance. We notified the IRS on August 21, 2013, that the newly revised processing instructions had not corrected the problem.

---

[21] A judgmental sample is a nonstatistical sample, the results of which cannot be used to project to the population.

Recommendations

The Commissioner, Wage and Investment Division, should:

Recommendation 3: Revise processes and procedures to ensure that all tax returns are verified for a required valid recipient TIN when an alimony deduction is claimed. These processes should include rejecting e-filed tax returns and sending paper tax returns to the IRS Error Resolution function for correspondence with the taxpayer.

> ***Management's Response:*** The IRS disagreed with this recommendation. The IRS stated that because the IRS does not possess the authority to deny the alimony deduction outside of deficiency procedures, the validation process is more efficiently performed within its Compliance function. The IRS also stated that the IRS Error Resolution function will either correspond with the taxpayer to obtain the TIN when the deduction meets certain criteria or assess a penalty for failure to provide the recipient TIN.

> ***Office of Audit Comment:*** In addition to disagreeing with our recommendation, the IRS also disagreed with our outcome measure of $137 million in potential revenue protected. As stated in our report, the IRS's current verification processes are not sufficient to identify all invalid recipient TINs. In addition, the lack of authority to deny an alimony deduction claim without conducting an examination does not preclude the IRS from notifying taxpayers that they are not compliant with the alimony reporting requirements. IRS examination program data show that the IRS examines very few tax returns for which there is an alimony reporting discrepancy. Establishing processes to communicate with all taxpayers who do not provide a valid recipient TIN provides the taxpayer the opportunity to voluntarily comply. Notifying taxpayers that the IRS is aware of their noncompliance may also deter taxpayers from making improper alimony deduction claims. As such, we believe our recommendation and the related outcome fairly represent the potential benefit the IRS could achieve by expanding efforts to obtain valid alimony recipient TINs for all alimony deduction claims.

Recommendation 4: Revise IRS processing instructions to ensure that penalties are assessed on applicable tax returns with an alimony deduction claim where a valid recipient TIN was not provided and ensure that the penalty is assessed in the correct amount.

> ***Management's Response:*** The IRS agreed with this recommendation. The IRS revised processing instructions on February 26, 2014, to ensure that all returns claiming a deduction for alimony paid are subject to the appropriate penalty provision when the alimony recipient's TIN is not provided and to ensure that the penalty is assessed in the correct amount. The IRS agreed with our outcome measure of $1.6 million in penalty assessments.

Appendix I

Detailed Objective, Scope, and Methodology

The overall objective of this review was to evaluate the alimony reporting gap and to assess controls the IRS has in place to promote reporting compliance. To accomplish our objective, we:

I.   Evaluated the alimony reporting gap for Tax Year[1] 2010.

A. Identified 567,887 individuals on the IRS Individual Return Transaction File[2] who claimed an alimony deduction in Tax Year 2010. We verified the accuracy and reliability of the data obtained from the sources above by comparing 60 tax returns (30 paper tax returns and 30 e-filed tax returns) to the returns originally filed by these 60 individuals. The data were determined to be sufficiently reliable for the purposes of the audit.

B. Identified 266,190 of the 567,887 tax returns in which the deduction amount did not agree with the income amount reported on the associated recipient tax return. To determine if a reporting discrepancy existed, we analyzed all 447,975 e-filed tax returns claiming an alimony deduction, the 84,562 paper tax returns claiming an alimony deduction above the examination dollar tolerance, and a statistically valid sample of 138 of the 35,350 paper tax returns claiming an alimony deduction below the examination dollar tolerance. We were unable to analyze all 35,350 tax returns with an alimony deduction below the examination dollar tolerance because the IRS does not capture the information needed to conduct such an analysis.

II. Assessed the effectiveness of the IRS's controls to detect and prevent erroneous alimony deduction claims.

A. Interviewed IRS management to identify the controls in place to identify and resolve discrepancies between amounts claimed as alimony deductions and amounts reported as alimony income.

B. Evaluated the adequacy of the IRS's process to identify tax returns claiming alimony deductions for potential examination. We reviewed a statistically valid sample of 385 tax returns that claimed an alimony deduction to determine if the tax returns were

---

[1] A 12-month accounting period for keeping records on income and expenses used as the basis for calculating the annual taxes due. For most individual taxpayers, the tax year is synonymous with the calendar year.

[2] A database the IRS maintains that contains information on the individual tax returns it receives.

identified for examination consideration. We also determined if the IRS examined the associated recipient tax return to verify income when appropriate.

C. Evaluated the effectiveness of the IRS's processes to detect and prevent alimony deduction claims with a missing or invalid recipient TIN. We identified the IRS's processes for identifying and preventing alimony deductions when the recipient TIN is missing or invalid. Using the Individual Return Transaction File and the National Account Profile,[3] we identified 6,500 Tax Year 2010 tax returns with a missing or invalid recipient TIN that were not detected by the IRS's processes.

D. Reviewed the Individual Return Transaction File for the 6,500 tax returns with a missing or invalid recipient TIN to determine if the IRS assessed the $50 penalty for a missing or invalid recipient TIN.

Sampling criteria

We selected and reviewed a statistically valid sample of 138 taxpayers from a population of 35,350 taxpayers filing a paper return claiming a deduction for alimony less than the IRS examination dollar tolerance in Tax Year 2010. A statistical sample was used to allow the results to be projected to the overall population. We relied on TIGTA's contract statistician to verify our sampling methods.

We selected our sample using a 95 percent confidence level, a ± 5 percent precision, and a 10 percent estimated error rate. Our review of the sample identified 79 tax returns in which alimony does not appear to have been correctly reported by the payer or the recipient. This resulted in a 57 percent error rate and a standard error deviation of ± 2,923 (17,314 to 23,160).

In addition, we selected a judgmental sample of 60 tax returns processed between June 28 and July 18, 2013, that met the IRS's existing penalty criteria to determine whether taxpayers had been assessed a penalty even though the recipient TIN was missing or invalid and the amount of the deduction was above the examination dollar tolerance.[4] The sample was selected to evaluate the adequacy of actions taken to address concerns we raised to the IRS on May 22, 2013, regarding the nonassessment of the alimony penalty when applicable. We used a judgmental sample because the process we were evaluating is systemic in nature and we were not projecting the results of the sample.

---

[3] The National Account Profile is a compilation of selected entity data from various master files and the Social Security Administration.

[4] We did not attempt to determine the population from which the sample was selected because the sample was used to verify a systemic process. In addition, the population was not needed as we did not intend to quantify the extent to which the IRS's corrective action addressed our concerns.

Internal controls methodology

Internal controls relate to management's plans, methods, and procedures used to meet their mission, goals, and objectives. Internal controls include the processes and procedures for planning, organizing, directing, and controlling program operations. They include the systems for measuring, reporting, and monitoring program performance. We determined that the following internal controls were relevant to our audit objective: the controls to identify discrepancies between alimony deductions claimed and alimony income reported and the controls to identify alimony deduction claims with a missing or invalid alimony recipient TIN. To evaluate these controls, we interviewed IRS management, reviewed IRS procedures, and analyzed individual tax returns claiming alimony deductions.

Appendix II

Major Contributors to This Report

Russell P. Martin, Acting Assistant Inspector General for Audit (Returns Processing and Account Services)
Kyle R. Andersen, Director
Deann L. Baiza, Director
Bill R. Russell, Audit Manager
W. George Burleigh, Lead Auditor
Laura P. Haws, Senior Auditor
Steven D. Stephens, Senior Auditor
Nikole L. Smith, Auditor
Joseph C. Butler, Information Technology Specialist
Kevin O'Gallagher, Information Technology Specialist

Report Distribution List

Commissioner C
Office of the Commissioner – Attn: Chief of Staff C
Deputy Commissioner for Services and Enforcement SE
Deputy Commissioner, Small Business/Self-Employed Division SE:S
Deputy Commissioner, Wage and Investment Division SE:W
Director, Compliance, Wage and Investment Division SE:W:CP
Director, Customer Account Services, Wage and Investment Division SE:W:CAS
Director, Examination, Small Business/Self-Employed Division SE:S:E
Director, Exam Policy, Small Business/Self-Employed Division SE:S:E:EP
Director, Reporting Compliance, Wage and Investment Division SE:W:CP:RC
Director, Submission Processing, Wage and Investment Division SE:W:CAS:SP
Chief, Program Evaluation and Improvement, Wage and Investment Division SE:W:S:PRA:PEI
Chief Counsel CC
National Taxpayer Advocate TA
Director, Office of Legislative Affairs CL:LA
Director, Office of Program Evaluation and Risk Analysis RAS:O
Office of Internal Control OS:CFO:CPIC:IC
Audit Liaisons:
    Program Manager, Policy and Strategic Planning, Communication, Liaison, and Disclosure, Small Business/Self-Employed Division SE:S:CLD:PSP
    Chief, Program Evaluation and Improvement, Wage and Investment Division SE:W:S:PRA:PEI

Outcome Measures

This appendix presents detailed information on the measurable impact that our recommended corrective actions will have on tax administration. These benefits will be incorporated into our Semiannual Report to Congress.

Type and Value of Outcome Measure:

- Revenue Protection – Potential; $351,826,543 in additional income tax assessed for 230,208 taxpayers during Tax Year 2010 as a result of noncompliance with alimony reporting requirements; $1,759,132,715 over five years (see page 4).

Methodology Used to Measure the Reported Benefit:

Using the IRS's Individual Return Transaction File,[1] we identified 567,887 tax returns that claimed an alimony deduction in Tax Year 2010. Our analysis of these 567,887 tax returns identified 266,190 tax returns in which it appears individuals claimed alimony deductions for which the corresponding income was either not reported on a recipient's tax return or the amount of the alimony income reported did not agree with the deduction taken. As such, there is a discrepancy of more than $2.3 billion in deductions claimed without a corresponding income reported.

To determine the estimated tax effect of unexamined discrepancies between alimony deductions claimed and alimony income reported, we first reduced the 266,190 tax returns we identified with questionable alimony deductions by the 6,500 returns with a missing or invalid recipient TIN because these tax returns are included in a separate outcome below. In addition, we reduced the 266,190 tax returns by the 10,870 returns that the IRS selected for examination to arrive at a total of 248,820 returns. We then applied the IRS examination rates noted on page 8 of this report to the 248,820 returns to estimate the number of tax returns where the alimony deduction and/or the nonreporting of alimony income are in error.

As of December 31, 2013, the IRS determined that adjustments were made on 56 percent of the Tax Year[2] 2010 returns with alimony deductions selected for examination. In addition, adjustments were made on 83 percent of the subsequent examinations made on the recipients' tax

---

[1] A database the IRS maintains that contains information on the individual tax returns it receives.

[2] A 12-month accounting period for keeping records on income and expenses used as the basis for calculating the annual taxes due. For most individual taxpayers, the tax year is synonymous with the calendar year.

returns. Applying these results to the 248,820 cases, we estimate that an additional 230,208 returns could be assessed additional tax.

248,820 x 56 percent = 139,339 tax returns with adjusted alimony deductions.

109,481[3] x 83 percent = 90,869 tax returns with adjusted alimony income.

139,339 + 90,869 = 230,208 total tax returns with potential adjustments resulting from the misreporting of alimony payments.

To compute the potential tax effect of the misreporting of alimony deductions, we computed the average difference between the amount deducted and the amount claimed as income for the 248,820 tax returns. We then multiplied this average difference by the average marginal tax rate (23 percent) based on the taxable income of the 139,339 tax returns with potential alimony deduction adjustments.

$2,128,089,529/248,820 = $8,553 average reporting discrepancy

$8,553 x 139,339 = $1,191,766,467

$1,191,766,467 x 23 percent = $274,106,287

To compute the potential tax effect of the misreporting of alimony income, we multiplied the 90,869 tax returns by the average reporting difference per tax return. We were unable to determine the average marginal tax rate for the tax returns with potential alimony income adjustments because we do not know what the total income claimed on these tax returns may be. As a result, we multiplied the estimated total reporting difference by a 10 percent tax rate (lowest rate in Tax Year 2010).

$2,128,089,529/248,820 = $8,553 average reporting discrepancy

$8,553 x 90,869 = $777,202,557

$777,202,557 x 10 percent = $77,720,256

We estimate the 230,208 taxpayers would be assessed additional income tax totaling $351,826,543 ($274,106,287 + $77,720,256) as a result of noncompliance with alimony reporting requirements. We estimate the taxpayers could be assessed $1,759,132,715 in additional income tax over the next five years ($351,826,543 x 5) as a result of noncompliance with alimony reporting requirements.

---

[3] 248,820 less the 139,339 tax returns we estimate the IRS will address through verification of the alimony deduction.

Type and Value of Outcome Measure:

• Revenue Protection – Potential; $27,485,640 in unpaid tax from questionable alimony deductions made on 6,500 taxpayers during Tax Year 2010 that did not include a valid recipient TIN; $137,428,200 over five years (see page 9).

Methodology Used to Measure the Reported Benefit:

Using the IRS's Individual Return Transaction File, we identified 567,887 tax returns that claimed an alimony deduction in Tax Year 2010. Our analysis of these 567,887 tax returns identified 3,771 tax returns that claimed an alimony deduction but did not provide an alimony recipient TIN as required. We also identified 2,729 tax returns where the recipient TIN provided was invalid.

To determine the tax effect of allowing these potentially erroneous deductions, we used an average of the 2010 tax rates based on the taxable income average of the exceptions from three segments: 1) the statistically valid sample[4] of 138 Tax Year 2010 paper-filed returns with deductions less than the examination dollar tolerance (noted above); 2) the population of Tax Year 2010 paper-filed returns with deductions equal to or greater than the examination dollar tolerance; and 3) the population of Tax Year 2010 e-filed returns with deductions for any amount. We then multiplied the tax rate by the projected dollar estimates of alimony deductions for returns with a missing recipient TIN and returns in which the recipient TIN was invalid. Figure 1 shows the computation of the estimated taxable income the IRS may have lost as a result of allowing alimony deductions with missing or invalid recipient TINs.

---

[4] We selected the sample using a 95 percent confidence level, a ± 5 percent precision, and a 10 percent estimated error rate to determine a point estimate of 1,537 returns.

Figure 1: Computation of Estimated Tax Revenue Lost as a Result of Missing or Invalid Alimony Recipient TINs in Tax Year 2010

3,771 Returns With Missing Recipient TINs

	Average Taxable Income	Applicable Tax Rate	Average Alimony Deduction	Number of Returns	Total Tax Effect
Paper/E-Filed ≥ Tolerance	$ 187,489	31%	$ 20,786	2,738	$ 17,642,741
E-Filed < Tolerance	$ 39,772	20%	$ 2,952	8	$ 4,723
Paper < Tolerance	$ 24,656	15%	$ 2,935	1,025	$ 451,256
				3,771	$ 18,098,720

2,729 Returns With Invalid Recipient TINs

	Average Taxable Income	Applicable Tax Rate	Average Alimony Deduction	Number of Returns	Total Tax Effect
Paper/E-Filed ≥ Tolerance	$ 116,348	27%	$ 20,152	1,645	$ 8,950,511
E-Filed < Tolerance	$ 49,423	21%	$ 2,738	572	$ 328,889
Paper < Tolerance	$ 4,421	10%	$ 2,100	512	$ 107,520
				2,729	$ 9,386,920

Total Returns	6,500
Tax Year 2010 Tax Effect	$ 27,485,640
Total 5-Year Tax Effect	$ 137,428,200

Source: TIGTA analysis of tax returns claiming alimony deductions in Tax Year 2010.

Type and Value of Outcome Measure:

- Increased Revenue – Potential; $324,900 in unassessed penalties for individuals who claimed alimony deductions but did not provide a valid alimony recipient TIN during Tax Year 2010; $1,624,500 over five years (see page 9).

Methodology Used to Measure the Reported Benefit:

We obtained IRS Individual Master File[5] data for the 6,500 Tax Year 2010 returns we identified that claimed an alimony deduction with a missing or invalid recipient TIN.[6] Using this data, we found that the IRS had not properly assessed the $50 penalty on 6,480 of these taxpayers. The IRS assessed a penalty on 20 of the 6,500 returns, but for only $5 per return. We provided the IRS, for analysis purposes, with a sample of the 6,500 tax returns in which the IRS had not assessed the penalty. IRS management agreed the penalty should have been assessed on these tax returns.

---

[5] The IRS database that maintains transactions or records of individual tax accounts.

[6] As noted in the body of the report, the 6,500 returns are based on a review of 4,963 actual returns and a statistically valid sample of 138 that accounted for an estimated 1,537 returns.

Based on IRS management's agreement that we properly identified tax returns that should have been assessed a $50 penalty, we project that 6,480 returns were not assessed penalties totaling $324,000 (6,480 x $50) and 20 returns were under assessed the penalty totaling $900 (20 x $45). Over a five-year period, this would result in more than $1.6 million in unassessed penalties ($324,900 x 5) for failure to provide a valid alimony recipient's TIN.

Appendix V

Example of a Soft Notice

Important message about your 2006 tax return

You may need to file an amended 2006 Form 1040X

We have received additional information from other sources (such as employers, financial institutions, etc.) that differs from the information you listed on your 2006 Form 1040.

What you need to do immediately

Review this notice and compare what you listed on your 2006 tax return to the amounts reported to the IRS by others.

If you agree with the information reported by other sources
- Complete an Amended U.S. Income Tax Return (Form 1040X) as soon as possible. Download Form 1040X and Instructions for Form 1040X from www.irs.gov, or call 1-800-829-3676 to request a copy.
- Send your completed 1040X to the same IRS address where you mailed your tax return. If you e-filed your tax return, you must mail a paper amended return. To find the correct mailing address, refer to the Instructions for Form 1040X.

If you don't agree with the information reported by other sources
- You don't need to respond to this notice.
- If you think your return is correct and there's a mistake in the information we received from other sources (employers, financial institutions, etc.), contact the sources directly to ask them to correct their records, as necessary.

Next Steps

- You should either file an amended return, or ask the other sources to correct their records.
- If you don't file an amended tax return or ask the other sources to correct their records, the errors will remain in your file, and you may continue to have similar reporting problems next year.

Continued on back...

Notice	CP2057
Tax Year	2006
Notice date	June 19, 2008
Social Security number	
Page 2 of 2	

Differences between your 2006 Form 1040 and information from other sources

This section tells you specifically what income information the IRS received about you from others (including your employers, banks, mortgage holders, etc.). This information doesn't match the information you reported on your tax return.

Use the table to review the data the IRS received from others and compare it to the information you reported on your tax return to understand where the difference(s) occurred.

Gross pension

Received from	Address	Account Information	Reported to IRS by others

Taxable Social Security benefits

Received from	Address	Account Information	Reported to IRS by others

Additional information

- Visit www.irs.gov/cp2057. You can also find the following online:
  - Amended U.S. Individual Tax Return (Form 1040X)
  - Instructions for Form 1040X
- For tax forms, instructions, and publications, visit www.irs.gov or call 1-800-TAX-FORM (1-800-829-3676).
- Keep this notice for your records.

If you need assistance, please don't hesitate to contact us.

Source: IRS.

Appendix VI

Management's Response to the Draft Report

DEPARTMENT OF THE TREASURY
INTERNAL REVENUE SERVICE
WASHINGTON, D.C. 20224

COMMISSIONER
SMALL BUSINESS/S ELF·EMPLOYED DIVISION

March 10, 2014

MEMORANDUM FOR MICHAEL E. MCKENNEY
                     ACTING DEPUTY INSPECTOR GENERAL FOR AUDIT

FROM: Karen Schiller /s/ Karen Schiller
                        Commissioner, Small Business/Self-Employed Division

SUBJECT: Draft Audit Report - Significant Discrepancies Exist Between
                        Alimony Deductions Claimed by Payers and Income Reported
                        by Recipients (Audit #201240016)

Thank you for the opportunity to review your draft report titled: "Significant Discrepancies Exist Between Alimony Deductions Claimed by Payers and Income Reported by Recipients". We will continue to make improvements to our processes to ensure consistent reporting between alimony recipients and alimony payers.

As your report noted, some individual federal tax returns contain a discrepancy between the alimony deductions claimed by payers and alimony income reported by recipients. We have implemented a strategy to address this gap which includes usage of a number of examination filters which we have developed and refined to isolate the most egregious returns for compliance activity. ********************2****************************** **2** *******2**************. We continue to monitor these examination filters to ensure our strategy adequately addresses the alimony reporting compliance gap.

In addition, our strategy to monitor those individuals who continue to misreport alimony deductions and/or income now includes procedures to assert penalties in all situations where the payer does not provide a recipient TIN. While we agree that sending soft notices is a valid alternative approach to address this issue, resource constraints limit our ability to test their impact at this time.

Internal Revenue Code (IRC) Section 215 requires the recipient of alimony payments to furnish their TIN to the alimony payer. They, in turn, are required to report that TIN on the tax return when they claim a deduction for alimony paid. The IRC does not make the alimony deduction dependent on the provision of the recipient's TIN. We, therefore, are

2

not able to revise our procedures to deny the alimony deduction if the TIN is not present. We have, however, revised our processing instructions to ensure the penalty for failure to provide the recipient TIN is assessed on all applicable returns.

Your report listed three outcome measures. We disagree with the first measure, revenue protection of more than $1.7 billion since we do not have the ability to audit all the returns cited. The measure does not consider the impact of the workload these cases would displace. We also disagree with the second measure, revenue protection of more than $137 million, because the IRS does not have the authority to deny an alimony deduction during return processing when the payer fails to furnish a valid recipient TIN. We agree with the third measure, increased revenue of $1.6 million, and will take steps to assess the penalty as appropriate.

Attached is a detailed response outlining our corrective actions to address your recommendations.

If you have any questions, please contact me, or a member of your staff may contact Kathryn D. Vaughan, Director, Campus Compliance Services at (404) 338-9116.

Attachment

Attachment

RECOMMENDATION 1:

The Commissioner, Small Business/Self-Employed Division, should work with the Commissioner, Wage and Investment Division to evaluate current examination selection filters to ensure that the filters do not inappropriately exclude potentially high-risk tax returns with questionable alimony deduction claims.

CORRECTIVE ACTION:

Filters were enhanced for Tax Year 2013 (Filing Season 2014). The Small Business/Self-Employed Division (SB/SE) will continue to work with the Wage & Investment Division (W&I) to review the current alimony filters and make improvements as necessary.

IMPLEMENTATION DATE:

October 15, 2015

RESPONSIBLE OFFICIAL(S):

Director, Campus Compliance Services, Small Business/Self-Employed Division
Director, Compliance, Wage and Investment Division

CORRECTIVE ACTION MONITORING PLAN:

The IRS will monitor this corrective action as part of our internal management system of controls.

RECOMMENDATION 2:

The Commissioner, Small Business/Self-Employed Division, should work with the Commissioner, Wage and Investment Division to develop a strategy that adequately addresses the significant alimony compliance gap. This strategy should include determining the net benefit of using soft notices as an alternative approach to address this issue as well as actions IRS plans to take with regard to individuals who continue to misreport alimony deductions and/or income.

CORRECTIVE ACTION:

The IRS currently has procedures in place to address the alimony compliance gap and will continue to review and improve our strategy as warranted. However, we do not believe it would be appropriate to pursue the soft notice approach at this time. While we agree that sending soft notices may be a valid approach in certain circumstances, resource constraints limit our ability to test their impact at this time. Soft notices would generate costs for printing, mailing, telephone calls, and working/evaluating responses. Instead, we will continue to improve our current strategy including making changes to the examination filters. The resulting inventory is reviewed for inclusion in our Examination work plan along with other priorities.

2

IMPLEMENTATION DATE:
N/A

RESPONSIBLE OFFICIAL(S):
N/A

CORRECTIVE ACTION MONITORING PLAN:
N/A

RECOMMENDATION 3:
The Commissioner, Wage and Investment Division, should revise processes and procedures to ensure that all tax returns are verified for a required valid recipient TIN when an alimony deduction is claimed. These processes should include rejecting e-filed tax returns and sending paper tax returns to the IRS Error Resolution function for correspondence with the taxpayer.

CORRECTIVE ACTION:
When taxpayers claim deductions for alimony paid and fail to provide the Taxpayer Identification Number (TIN) of the alimony recipient, the Error Resolution function will either correspond with the taxpayer to obtain the number, when the deduction meets certain criteria, or assess a penalty for failure to provide the recipient TIN. This process is applied to both paper and electronic returns. Because the authority to assess the penalty for failure to provide the recipient TIN does not extend to permit the IRS to deny the alimony deduction outside of deficiency procedures, the validation process is more efficiently performed within our Compliance function. Therefore, we do not intend to implement the recommended actions.

IMPLEMENTATION DATE:
N/A

RESPONSIBLE OFFICIAL(S):
N/A

CORRECTIVE ACTION MONITORING PLAN:
N/A

RECOMMENDATION 4:
Revise IRS processing instructions to ensure that penalties are assessed on applicable tax returns with an alimony deduction claim where a valid recipient TIN was not provided and ensure that the penalty is assessed in the correct amount.

3

CORRECTIVE ACTION:
Processing instructions in Internal Revenue Manual section 3.12.3.62.5.3, *Individual Income Tax Returns*, were revised on February 26, 2014, to ensure all returns claiming a deduction for alimony paid are subject to the appropriate penalty provision when the alimony recipient's TIN is not provided. The procedural update also clarified input instructions to ensure the penalty is assessed in the correct amount.

IMPLEMENTATION DATE:
Completed

RESPONSIBLE OFFICIAL(S):
Director, Submission Processing, Customer Account Services, Wage and Investment Division

CORRECTIVE ACTION MONITORING PLAN:
N/A

www.ingramcontent.com/pod-product-compliance
Lightning Source LLC
Chambersburg PA
CBHW080532190526
45169CB00008B/3134